A Taste of Singapore

Edited by
Kenneth Mitchell

Singapore, Dec. 8, 1983

Dear Steve, Anne & Dove,
This is why I sent you
those chiles. Have fun
cooking — this food is the
greatest. Merry Xmas!

Love,
Mike

This edition published by
Four Corners Publishing Co. (Far East) Ltd.,
257, Gloucester Road, Hong Kong.
for
Oracle Book Distributors
Copyright © 1980, Kenneth Mitchell
ISBN 85623016 2
Typeset by Filmset Limited
Printed in Hong Kong

D1157292

Introduction

The first person to describe Singapore as 'The Crossroads of Asia' no doubt had in mind its geographical location, situated as it is practically on the equator at the very heart of South East Asia with easy accessibility to China and Japan in the north and the Indian sub-continent in the west. Yet how aptly this same phrase may be used to introduce the culinary delights of this colourful and compact Island State where the visitor is greeted with an amazing variety of tangy aromas and spicy flavours which so accurately reflect the varied racial origins of today's Singaporeans.

In the kitchens of Singapore, where truly East meets East, the many styles of Chinese cooking compete with the richly spiced foods of the Indians, Malays and Indonesians. Here, a multitude of cooks manage not only to successfully reproduce the traditional fare of their ancestors but also to create new and exciting recipes by 'blending cuisines' like others elsewhere blend spices.

Since the people of Chinese origin predominate, so does their food, and dishes from most of the regions of China are served both in the homes and in the restaurants. From the highly esteemed Cantonese flavours to the hot and spicy dishes of Szechuan; from the classical cooking of Imperial Peking to the more simple food of the wandering Hakka people. And: Hokkien; Hainanese; Hunanese; all distinctive styles of cooking and all to be found in Singapore as part of the 'local' scene. Then there are all the marvellous curries: The coconut flavoured curries of nearby Malaysia and Indonesian; the biting curries of southern India and the more subtle tastes of the north; and even the 'tiffin' dishes which the English introduced to the region more than a hundred years ago. Then there is Nonya cooking, a style of cuisine created by the early settlers from China who adapted the readily available local ingredients (particularly the spices) to their own styles of cooking. And last, but certainly not least, there are the many splendoured delights of the Singapore food stalls; so varied, numerous and 'different' they defy description in this small space. Suffice it to say that here, like perhaps nowhere else in the world, can be found food that will delight the appreciative and demanding palate of even the most well travelled gourmand.

Because of this great variety of food, it was difficult to decide how best to group the recipes in this book. My first choice was for an ethnic division but then the question was where to include such dishes as CHILLI CRAB, MULLIGATAWNEY SOUP and RUM RAISIN ICE-CREAM. Then again, should there be a separate section for the hawker's food? Certainly at one time this would have been essential because it stood alone and was only available at the roadside stalls. But now, because of its increasing popularity with visitors (it has always been popular with locals) many of the dishes are offered as regular fare in the various ethnic restaurants and indeed some large hotels have set aside areas specializing in this style of food. So finally, in spite of the fact that Asian meals are not generally served in courses as in the West, I decided on the well-tried and simple format of: soups; seafoods; poultry; meats and desserts with a special section of local favourites. In line with this thinking I have indicated a number of servings with each recipe, but again it should be remembered that a typical meal will generally consist of a number of dishes being shared by all the diners, so one's own judgement becomes more important than my suggestion.

Weights and Measures

Most of the weights and measures throughout the book are in metric but any ingredient under 25 grams (25 g) or 25 millilitres (25 ml) has been indicated in teaspoons. For those who continue to think and work in Imperial measures there is a quick and simple conversion to keep in mind. That is to take 25 grams as being equal to 1 ounce and 25 millilitres to 1 fluid ounce. However this is not a precise conversion and, while quite satisfactory for small quantities, tends to become less practical as weights and measures increase. The table below shows the nearest gram/millilitre equivalent for 1 to 20 ounces/fluid ounces and indicates the difference between the Imperial and U.S. pint. A measuring cup is roughly the equivalent of 225 millilitres.

Ounces/fluid ounces	Approx. g. and ml. to nearest whole figure	Ounces/fluid ounces	Approx. g. and ml. to nearest whole figure
1	28	11	311
2	57	12	340
3	85	13	368
4	113	14	396
5	142	15	428
6	170	16 (American pint)	456
7	198	17	484
8	226	18	512
9	255	19	541
10	283	20 (Imperial pint)	569

In this edition I've tried to present a fair cross section of the variety of Asian foods which go to make up the diet of the very fortunate Singaporean but obviously with such limited space it has not been possible to be anywhere near comprehensive. Certain omissions have been deliberate because the recipes appear in other books in this series. On the other hand I offer no apology for including some recipes which do appear in those other books. For one things they were collected from different sources and therefore are not exactly the same in each case, but the other far more important reason is that to omit the likes of: SATAY; STEAMBOAT and BEEF RENDANG (included in A Taste of Malaysia) as well as: SZECHUAN SOUP and SWEET AND SOUR PORK (included in A Taste of Hong Kong) would be failing to accurately portray the true TASTE OF SINGAPORE.

May your pleasure from this 'TASTE' be as great as mine.

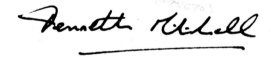

'Fatty's' in Albert Street is one of Singapore's best known roadside restaurants.

Soups

Wan Tun Soup

24 frozen wan tun wrappers
250 g fresh pork
100 g fresh shrimps
6 water chestnuts
salt
white pepper
pinch monosodium glutamate
1 egg-white, beaten
½ small Chinese cabbage
1 litre chicken stock

serves 4

Place the wan tun wrappers in a warming oven to thaw out then lay out flat on a lightly greased pastry board. Cut away excess fat from the pork, shell and de-vein the shrimps and skin the water chestnuts. Mince together the pork, shrimps and chestnuts and season with salt, white pepper and monosodium glutamate. Spoon a little of the mixture on to each wrapper and fold into triangle shapes. Seal edges with the beaten egg-white. In a large saucepan bring the stock to the boil. Cut the cabbage leaves into 50 mm lengths, add these to the stock and continue to boil rapidly for 2 minutes. Transfer the vegetable to individual serving bowls and add the wan tuns to the stock. When they rise to the surface, remove, drain and place in the serving bowls. Adjust the seasoning of the stock, continue to boil for a further minute then pour into the bowls.

Chicken & Sweet Corn Soup

100 g white chicken meat
1 egg white
½ teaspoon salt
¼ teaspoon white pepper
pinch monosodium glutamate
1 litre chicken stock
200 g can sweet corn
25 ml Chinese wine
2 teaspoons light soya sauce
1 teaspoon dark soya sauce
1 teaspoon sesame oil
2 teaspoons cornstarch
25 g shredded cooked ham

serves 4

Chop the chicken meat very finely. Beat the egg-white lightly, season with salt, white pepper and monosodium glutamate, pour over the chicken and allow to stand for 20 minutes. In a large saucepan bring the stock to the boil, add the sweet corn, Chinese wine, soya sauce and sesame oil and simmer for 3 minutes. Then add the chicken together with the egg marinade and continue to cook over a moderate heat for a further 2–3 minutes, stirring occasionally. Mix the cornstarch with a small quantity of cold water and stir into the soup to thicken slightly. Transfer to a soup tureen and sprinkle the shredded ham on top.

Szechuan Soup

4 dried Chinese mushrooms
50 g bamboo shoot
50 g cucumber
2 squares chilli beancurd
2 fresh red chillies
20 mm knob fresh ginger
100 g shrimps
100 g roasted pork
25 ml vegetable oil
1.5 litres chicken stock
2 teaspoons light soya sauce
2 teaspoons dark soya sauce
25 ml vinegar
25 ml Chinese wine
1 teaspoon freshly ground white pepper
salt to taste
2 teaspoons cornstarch
1 egg
1 teaspoon chilli oil

serves 6

Soak the mushrooms in warm water for 30 minutes then discard the hard stems and shred the caps. Shred all the other vegetables. Shell and de-vein the shrimps and cut in half, lengthways. Shred the pork. Heat the oil in a large pan, add the vegetables, the shrimps and the pork and stir-fry for 2 minutes then pour in the stock and bring to the boil. Add soya sauce, vinegar, Chinese wine, freshly ground white pepper and salt to taste, lower heat and simmer for a further 3 minutes. Mix the cornstarch with a small quantity of cold water and add to the soup to thicken slightly. Beat the egg and stir into the soup just prior to transferring to a tureen. Heat the chilli oil and sprinkle this over the soup then serve immediately.

Mulligatawny Soup

2 onions
2 carrots
1 cooking apple
50 g butter
50 g all-purpose flour
50 g curry powder
1½ litres chicken stock
2 bay leaves
2 sprigs parsley
2 sprigs thyme
25 g tomato paste
salt to taste
freshly ground white pepper
25 g mango chutney
50 g cooked rice
75 ml fresh cream

serves 4–6

Dice the onions, carrots and apple. Melt the butter in a large saucepan, add the onion and carrot and sauté for 2–3 minutes until the onion becomes soft. Add the flour and curry powder and stir fry over a moderate heat for 2 minutes. Pour in the stock, stir well and bring to the boil. Make a bouquet garni of the bay leaves, parsley and thyme and add to the stock together with the tomato paste and diced apple. Season to taste with salt and freshly ground white pepper, cover the pan, lower heat and simmer gently for 1 hour. Then remove from the heat, discard the bouquet garni and allow the soup to cool. Pour through a coarse sieve into a fresh saucepan, pressing the vegetables with a wooden spoon. Just prior to serving return the soup to the stove and bring back to the boil. Chop the chutney into tiny pieces and add this to the pan together with the cooked rice. Stir well and let simmer for a further minute then stir in the cream and immediately transfer to a soup tureen.

Seafoods

Seafood Steamboat

12 medium size prawns
12 medium size cuttlefish
400 g garoupa fillets
400 g cockles
24 fishballs*
24 quail eggs
lettuce leaves
300 g Chinese spinach
400 g Chinese cabbage
2 pieces fish maw
2 litres clear stock
salt to taste
freshly ground black pepper
pinch monosodium glutamate
1 teaspoon sesame oil

Sauce:
10 fresh red chillies
15 mm knob fresh ginger
2 cloves garlic
25 ml fresh lime juice
25 ml light soya sauce
25 ml chicken stock

serves 6

Prepare the fish as follows. Shell and de-vein the prawns, cut along the back and fold open. Remove the heads and backbone from the cuttlefish and cut into 15 mm lengths. Cut the garoupa fillets into 20 mm squares. Remove the shells from the cockles. Cook the fishballs in rapidly boiling salted water for 5 minutes. Wash all the seafood and drain thoroughly. Next boil the quail eggs for 8–10 minutes then soak in cold water and remove shells. Wash and drain the lettuce leaves and place on a large serving platter. Arrange the seafoods and the quail eggs on top of the lettuce and set on the table. Wash the spinach, cut the leaves into 50 mm lengths and arrange on a separate plate. Boil the cabbage for 3–4 minutes then drain thoroughly. Soak the fish maw in warm water for 20 minutes then drain and cut into small pieces. In a large saucepan bring the stock to the boil, add the cabbage and fish maw and season with salt, freshly ground black pepper and monosodium glutamate. Allow to boil rapidly for 2 minutes then transfer to a steamboat (stove and kettle) and place in the centre of the table together with the seafoods, spinach and hot chilli sauce.

Note that the heat from the stove should be just sufficient to keep the stock simmering while the individual diners cook their own food. Finally the enriched stock should be served into soup bowls to finish the meal.

To make the sauce: chop the shallots, garlic and garlic very finely, mix well with the fresh lime juice, soya sauce and chicken stock.

*To make fishballs use fillets of wolf herring or Spanish mackeral. Make certain all the small bones have been removed then chop the fish very finely. Season to taste and mix with cornstarch and a little water. Roll into small balls, about 15 mm in diameter, and place in a bowl of iced water. Set aside in the refrigerator for 1 hour and dry throughly before using. Besides being used in the Steamboat the fishballs can also be used in a soup.

Seafood Steamboat photographed at **Waterfall Restaurant**, Shangri La Hotel

Deep Fried Prawns with Chilli & Ginger

500 g fresh prawns
½ teaspoon salt
¼ teaspoon white pepper
50 ml Chinese wine
1 egg-white
25 g cornstarch
4 fresh red chillies
20 mm knob fresh ginger
1 clove garlic
vegetable oil for deep frying
25 ml light soya sauce
25 ml vinegar
25 g sugar
pinch monosodium glutamate

serves 4–6

Shell and de-vein the prawns and place in a shallow dish. Season with salt, white pepper and half the Chinese wine and allow to stand for 20 minutes. Beat the egg-white, mix with the cornstarch and pour over the prawns, tossing well to ensure an even coating. Chop the chillies and ginger and crush the garlic. Heat the oil in a wok and deep fry the prawns until golden brown then remove, drain thoroughly and set aside. Pour off most of the oil from the wok, add the chilli, ginger and garlic and sauté over a fairly high heat for 3–4 minutes. Then add the soya sauce, vinegar, remaining Chinese wine, sugar and monosodium glutamate and stir to blend thoroughly. Finally replace the prawns and stir fry for 30 seconds, then serve immediately.

Cathay 'Gold Coin' Prawns

600 g fresh prawns
1 teaspoon salt
½ teaspoon white pepper
pinch monosodium glutamate
2 egg-whites
2 teaspoons cornstarch
½ teaspoon baking soda
100 g breadcrumbs
100 g white bread
oil for deep frying

serves 6

Shell and de-vein the prawns and rinse in cold water. Season with salt, white pepper and monosodium glutamate and leave in a colander to dry. Then pat to dry thoroughly and chop very finely. In a mixing bowl beat the egg-whites lightly, add the prawn, cornstarch, baking soda and breadcrumbs and mix well. Place in the refrigerator for 1 hour. Meanwhile, remove the crusts from the bread, cut into thick slices then chop into tiny dice. Divide the prawn mixture and shape into balls, approximate 25 mm in diameter. Coat the prawn balls with the finely chopped bread and press into flat coin shapes. Heat the oil in a wok until smoking then deep fry the prawn coins until the outside is golden and crispy. Remove from the oil and drain well before serving.

Deep Fried Cuttlefish

600 g small cuttlefish
3 red chillies
2 cloves garlic
1 teaspoon bicarbonate of soda
1 litre vegetable oil
50 ml peanut oil
2 teaspoons sugar
50 ml tomato sauce
2 teaspoons Worcestershire sauce
salt to taste
freshly ground black pepper
lettuce leaves
1 teaspoon finely chopped parsley

serves 4

Clean the cuttlefish and remove the head and backbone. Cut the chillies into julienne strips and crush the garlic. Bring a pan of water to the boil, add the bicarbonate of soda and boil the cuttlefish for 10 minutes. Then pour into a colander, drain and pat dry with a paper towel. Heat the vegetable oil in a wok until it is smoking then deep fry the cuttlefish for 2–3 minutes until the outside skin is crispy. Remove and drain off all excess oil. Clean the wok and heat the peanut oil then add the chilli and garlic and stir-fry for 3 minutes. Add the sugar, tomato sauce, Worcestershire sauce, salt and freshly ground black pepper and stir to blend thoroughly. Finally return the cuttlefish and cook for a further minute, stirring frequently. To serve arrange crispy lettuce leaves on a serving plate, place the cuttlefish on top and garnish with finely chopped parsley.

Fried Mussels in Black Bean & Chilli Sauce

1 kilo fresh mussels
100 ml vegetable oil
50 g preserved soya beans
½ green pepper
3 fresh red chillies
20 mm knob fresh ginger
2 cloves garlic
25 g sugar
1 teaspoon salt
freshly ground black pepper
200 ml chicken stock
25 g cornstarch
1 teaspoon finely chopped parsley

serves 4

Wash the mussels under cold running water and scrub with a stiff brush. Leave to soak in cold water for 20 minutes then rub dry. Heat 75 g of the oil in a frying pan and stir-fry the mussels until the shells open. Set the mussels aside and clean the pan. Crush the soya beans and mix with a little cold water. Cut the green pepper, red chillies and ginger into thin strips and crush the garlic. Heat the remaining oil in the pan and sauté the garlic for 2 minutes then add the soya bean, green pepper, chilli and ginger and continue to cook over a moderate heat for a further 2 minutes. Add the mussels, sugar, salt and freshly ground black pepper and pour in the chicken stock. Bring to the boil, then lower heat and simmer for 2 minutes. Mix the cornstarch with a small quantity of cold water, add to the pan and stir until the sauce thickens slightly. Serve in individual clay pots and garnish with chopped parsley.

Steamed Pomfret Rolls

1 pomfret, about 600 g
½ teaspoon salt
¼ teaspoon white pepper
100 g cooked ham
20 mm knob fresh ginger
4 spring onions
fresh coriander leaves
1 teaspoon peanut oil

serves 4

Scale and clean the fish. Carefully remove the fillets and extract all the small bones but leave the backbone, head and tail intact. Slice the fillets of fish into 40 mm lengths, flatten slightly with the side of a knife and season with salt and white pepper. Cut the ham, ginger and 3 of the spring onions into julienne strips and chop the remaining spring onion and the fresh coriander leaves. Next place one strip each of ham, ginger and spring onion on top of each fish fillet and roll up leaving a little of the stuffing showing on both ends. When all the rolls have been completed arrange them attractively on the carcass of the pomfret and sprinkle the peanut oil on top. Place the fish in a steamer and cook over a medium heat for 7–8 minutes. When cooked transfer to a serving dish and garnish with the chopped spring onion and coriander.

Steamed Pomfret Rolls photographed at **Hilton Hotel**

Deep Fried Fish with Sweet & Sour Sauce

1 pomfret, about 600 g
½ teaspoon salt
½ teaspoon black pepper
2 eggs
50 g cornstarch
oil for deep frying
1 brown onion
1 green pepper
2 fresh red chillies
15 mm knob fresh ginger
1 clove garlic
25 ml Chinese wine
25 ml light soya sauce
25 ml vinegar
150 ml fish stock
50 g sugar
75 g canned pineapple chunks

serves 2

Scale and clean the fish but do not remove the head or tail. With a sharp knife score the skin about six places and rub in the salt and black pepper. Beat the eggs and mix with three quarters of the cornstarch. Pour the mixture over the fish and set on one side for 20 minutes. Heat the oil in a wok until it starts to smoke then deep fry the fish for 6–8 minutes, until it is cooked and the skin is golden and crispy. Remove the fish from the pan, drain off excess oil and keep warm. Chop the onion, green pepper, chillies, ginger and garlic. Pour away most of the oil from the wok, add all the vegetables and sauté for 3–4 minutes then add the Chinese wine, soya sauce, vinegar and sugar and adjust seasonings to taste. Stir until the sugar has completely dissolved then add the pieces of pineapple and simmer gently for a further 2 minutes. Finally mix the remaining cornstarch with a small quantity of cold water, add to the sauce and stir to thicken slightly. To serve, arrange the fish on a serving plate and pour the sauce on top.

Steamed Garoupa with Ginger

1 whole garoupa, about 600 g
½ teaspoon salt
½ teaspoon white pepper
20 mm knob fresh ginger
3 spring onions
25 ml light soya sauce
25 ml peanut oil

serves 2

Clean and scale the fish but do not remove the head or tail. With a sharp knife make an incision along the underside and remove the backbone. Season the fish with salt and white pepper and set aside for 30 minutes. Chop the ginger and spring onions very finely, mix with the soya sauce and stuff into the prepared pocket of the fish. Place on a steamer rack. Heat the peanut oil and pour over the fish. Place the rack over boiling water, cover and cook for approximately 10 minutes.

Deep Fried Garoupa

400 g fillets of garoupa
2 spring onions
15 mm knob fresh ginger
50 ml Chinese wine
1 teaspoon sesame oil
1 teaspoon sugar
½ teaspoon salt
¼ teaspoon white pepper
pinch monosodium glutamate
2 eggs
125 g all-purpose flour
1 teaspoon baking soda
oil for deep frying

serves 4

Make certain the fillets are completely free of bones then cut into pieces, about 60 mm × 25 mm, and place in a shallow dish. Chop the spring onions and ginger very finely, mix with the Chinese wine, sesame oil, sugar, salt, white pepper and monosodium glutamate and pour over the fish. Set aside for 30 minutes. Break the eggs into a mixing bowl, add the flour, baking soda and sufficient cold water to make a thin, smooth batter. Heat the oil in a wok until it begins to smoke. Remove the fish from the marinade, coat with the batter and deep fry until the outside is golden and crispy. Served with green vegetables.

Fish Curry

500 g fish fillets
1 teaspoon salt
½ teaspoon white pepper
1 large brown onion
20 mm knob fresh ginger
2 cloves garlic
2 teaspoons coriander powder
2 teaspoons cumin powder
1 teaspoon turmeric powder
1 teaspoon paprika
2 teaspoons sugar
50 ml vegetable oil
100 ml chicken stock

serves 4

Make certain all the bones are removed from the fillets then cut into bite size cubes and season with salt and white pepper. Chop the onion, ginger and garlic and pound together with all the spices, the sugar and a small quantity of cold water. (The result should be a thick spice paste.) Heat the oil in a large pan and fry the spice paste for 3-4 minutes, stirring constantly, then add the fish and the stock and bring to the boil. Cover the pan, lower heat and simmer until the fish is fully cooked. Remove cover from the pan, increase heat and let liquid reduce by one quarter. Serve with steamed rice and vegetables.

Fried Fish with Soya Bean Sauce

600 g fish fillets
50 g cornstarch
vegetable oil for deep frying
75 g preserved soya beans
25 g sugar
2 spring onions
20 mm knob fresh ginger
1 clove garlic
25 ml peanut oil
salt to taste
freshly ground black pepper
pinch monosodium glutamate
1 teaspoon sesame oil

serves 4

Make certain the fillets are completely free of bones then dust with the cornstarch. Heat the vegetable oil in a large pan and deep fry the fish until it is cooked then remove from the oil, drain and set aside in a warm place. Crush the soya beans, place in a saucepan together with the sugar and pour in 250 ml of cold water. Bring to the boil then simmer for 2–3 minutes. Chop the spring onions and ginger and crush the garlic. Heat the peanut oil in a wok and sauté the ginger and garlic for 2 minutes then add the spring onion, pour in the soya bean mixture and season with salt, freshly ground black pepper and monosodium glutamate. Bring back to the boil and cook for a further 3 minutes, stirring frequently. To serve cut the fish into small pieces, arrange on a serving plate and pour the sauce on top. Finally heat the sesame oil and sprinkle over the fish.

Fried Pomfret with Vegetables

600 g pomfret fillets
1 teaspoon salt
½ teaspoon white pepper
vegetable oil for deep frying
100 g Chinese cabbage
50 g carrots
50 g canned golden mushrooms
50 g canned bamboo shoot
2 cloves garlic
25 ml peanut oil
25 ml light soya sauce
25 ml oyster sauce
25 g sugar
2 teaspoons cornstarch

serves 4

Make sure the fillets are completely free of bones then season with salt and white pepper. Heat the oil in a wok and deep fry the fish until cooked then remove, drain and set aside. Shred the cabbage and carrots, cook for 3–4 minutes in boiling water then drain and set aside. Shred the mushrooms and bamboo shoot and crush the garlic. Heat the peanut oil in a pan and sauté the garlic for 3–4 minutes then add the vegetables and cook for a further 2 minutes, stirring frequently. Add the soya sauce, oyster sauce and sugar and pour in 100 ml of cold water. Bring to the boil, add the fish and cook for 1 minute. Mix the cornstarch with a small quantity of cold water and stir into the sauce to thicken then serve immediately.

Poultry

Tandoori Chicken

2 small chickens, about 600 g each
3 cloves garlic
1 fresh red chilli
20 mm knob fresh ginger
½ teaspoon salt
¼ teaspoon saffron powder
25 ml fresh lemon juice
200 ml natural yoghurt
2 teaspoons coriander powder
1 teaspoon cumin powder
¼ teaspoon anise powder
¼ teaspoon cayenne pepper
1 teaspoon paprika
50 g ghee

serves 4–6

Clean and prepare the chickens and remove the skin. Make sure the chickens are dried thoroughly then, with a sharp knife, make slits in the thighs and breasts. Chop the garlic, chilli and ginger and pound together with the salt, saffron powder and a small quantity of cold water to form a smooth paste. Rub this paste into the flesh of the chickens and put them to one side for 30 minutes. In the meantime mix the yoghurt with the coriander, cumin, anise, cayenne pepper, paprika and any remaining spice paste. Arrange the chickens in a casserole dish, add the yoghurt mixture and place in a refrigerator to marinate for at least 12 hours. After removing from the marinade baste the chickens with ghee, place on a rotisserie and cook in a moderately hot oven for 15–20 minutes then lower the heat slightly, baste again with ghee and continue to cook until the chickens are tender. Serve with naan, a flat Indian bread, and an onion and tomato salad.

Note: Some Indian restaurants have special Tandoori ovens made of clay and heated by hot coals. The chickens are then placed on long skewers which are lowered into the oven and without doubt this gives a flavour that is impossible to match in the home kitchen. Fish is sometimes also cooked by this method although the traditional tandoori dish is certainly chicken. Where the oven is available Naan, the bread mentioned above, is cooked on the sides.

Tandoori photographed at **The Islander Restaurant,** Hyatt Hotel

Chilli Chicken with Green Peppers

500 g chicken meat
1 egg
25 g cornstarch
½ teaspoon salt
¼ teaspoon white pepper
pinch monosodium glutamate
4 fresh red chillies
1 green pepper
2 shallots
1 clove garlic
50 g preserved black beans
500 ml vegetable oil
25 ml light soya sauce
25 ml Chinese wine
100 ml chicken stock
1½ teaspoons sesame oil

serves 4

Cut the chicken into bite size pieces and place in a shallow dish. Beat the egg, mix with the cornstarch and season with salt, white pepper and monosodium glutamate. Chop the chillies, green pepper and shallots and crush the garlic. Pound the black beans very slightly. Heat the oil in a wok, add the chicken and stir fry over a very high heat for 1 minute. Remove the chicken and set to one side and pour away most of the oil from the wok. Place the shallot and garlic in the wok and sauté for 3–4 minutes then add the chilli, green pepper and black beans and continue to cook fairly rapidly for a further 2–3 minutes, stirring frequently. Replace the pieces of chicken, pour in the soya sauce, Chinese wine and stock and adjust seasonings to taste. Bring to the boil then lower heat and simmer until the stock has almost completely reduced. Transfer to a serving dish. Heat the sesame oil in a small pan and sprinkle over the chicken just prior to serving.

Almond Chicken with Pineapple Sauce

4 chicken breasts
4 chicken thighs
2 eggs
1 teaspoon salt
½ teaspoon white pepper
2 teaspoons light soya sauce
2 teaspoons Chinese wine
100 g cornstarch
200 g almonds
oil for deep frying

Sauce:
400 ml chicken stock
100 ml can pineapple juice
1 teaspoon honey
75 g can pineapple chunks
1 teaspoon sugar
¼ teaspoon salt

serves 6

Remove all bones from the pieces of chicken and flatten with a knife. Beat the eggs, add the salt, white pepper, soya sauce, Chinese wine and 25 g of the cornstarch and mix thoroughly. Marinate the chicken in the mixture for 30 minutes. Shell the almonds and chop coarsely. Remove the chicken from the marinade and place, skin downwards, on a flat surface. Sprinkle the chopped almonds on top and with the hands press firmly into the flesh of the chicken then coat with the remaining cornstarch. Heat the oil in a wok and deep fry the chicken until cooked and golden. Then remove and drain off all excess oil. To serve, cut the chicken into bite size pieces, arrange on a large plate and pour the pineapple sauce on top. To make the sauce: bring the stock to the boil, reduce slightly then add all the other ingredients and stir to blend. Simmer over a low heat for 2 minutes before serving.

Dried Curry Chicken

1 fresh chicken, about 1.5 kilos
50 g curry powder
2 large brown onions
4 shallots
25 mm knob fresh ginger
2 cloves garlic
2 stalks lemon grass
75 ml thick coconut milk
25 ml vegetable oil
1 teaspoon chilli powder
1 teaspoon turmeric powder
1 teaspoon ground candlenut
freshly ground white pepper
salt to taste
150 ml thin coconut milk

serves 6

Clean and prepare the chicken, remove the skin and cut into serving size pieces. Coat the chicken with curry powder and set aside. Chop the onions, shallots, ginger, garlic and lemon grass. In a large saucepan bring the thick coconut milk to the boil and boil rapidly until the liquid has nearly all evaporated leaving an oily substance at the bottom of the pan. Add to this the vegetable oil and re-heat. Add the onion, shallot and garlic and stir-fry for 3 minutes then add the ginger, lemon grass, chilli powder, turmeric powder, ground candlenut, freshly ground white pepper and salt. Stir to blend thoroughly then add the pieces of chicken and pour in the thin coconut milk. Bring almost to boiling point and cook until the chicken is tender and most of the liquid has evaporated.

Serve with steamed rice and 'tiffin' side dishes such as grated coconut, chopped peanuts, diced pineapple and tomato and mango chutney.

Ayam Panggang

1 fresh chicken, about 1.5 kilos
6 shallots
3 cloves garlic
1 large brown onion
2 fresh red chillies
1 teaspoon ground candlenut
1 teaspoon coriander powder
1 teaspoon white pepper
salt to taste
25 g palm sugar
50 ml tamarind water
400 ml thick coconut milk
25 ml peanut oil

serves 4–6

Clean and prepare the chicken and cut into serving size pieces. Put aside 2 shallots and 1 clove of garlic. Chop the brown onion, red chillies and remaining shallots and garlic and pound these together with the candlenut, coriander, white pepper, salt and sugar. Combine with the tamarind water and coconut milk and stir well to blend and form a thick paste. Rub some of this paste over the pieces of chicken and set aside for 1 hour. Then cook the chicken under a hot grill or on an open charcoal fire. Pour the remaining paste into a wok and bring almost to boiling point then lower heat and simmer for 4–5 minutes, stirring constantly. Arrange the pieces of chicken on a serving plate and spoon the spiced sauce over the top. Finally chop the remaining shallots and garlic, fry in the oil until golden and crispy and sprinkle over the chicken.

Pigeons Baked in Salt

2 pigeons, about 350 g each
4 shallots
4 spring onions
20 mm knob fresh ginger
1 clove garlic
50 ml Chinese wine
25 ml light soya sauce
25 ml dark soya sauce
½ teaspoon anise powder
salt to taste
freshly ground white pepper
monosodium glutamate
2 sheets mulberry paper
2 kilos rock salt

serves 2

Clean and prepare the pigeons. Chop the shallots, spring onions, ginger and garlic, all very finely, and mix with the Chinese wine, soya sauce, anise powder, salt, white pepper and monosodium glutamate. Rub the mixture over the outside of the pigeons and stuff the remainder inside. Set aside for 1 hour then wrap the birds individually in sheets of well-greased mulberry paper. Heat the rock salt in a wok until it is extremely hot then bury the birds in the salt, place a cover on the wok and leave on a low heat for 10–12 minutes. Remove the birds and re-heat the salt then repeat the cooking process for a further 10 minutes. To serve, unwrap the pigeons, remove the stuffing, and chop into bite size pieces.

Hin's Smoked Duck

1 fat duck, approximately 2 kilos
1 teaspoon Chinese five-spice powder
1 teaspoon sugar
½ teaspoon salt
½ teaspoon white pepper
20 ml honey
1 teaspoon fresh lemon juice

Sauce:
50 ml chilli sauce
½ teaspoon grated fresh ginger
1 teaspoon dark soya sauce
dash garlic juice
1 teaspoon sugar

serves 4

Prepare the duck and clean thoroughly. Secure the wings in order that they will not open during cooking. Mix the Chinese five-spice powder, sugar, salt and white pepper and rub the mixture inside the duck. In a saucepan bring 100 ml of water to the boil, add the honey and lemon juice and stir until the honey has completely dissolved. Allow the syrup to cool slightly then rub all over the outside of the duck. Tie a string around the duck's neck and hang in a warm and draughty place to dry. Preferably the duck should be then cooked in a charcoal oven but if this is not available, place on a spit and cook over an open charcoal fire, turning frequently. Serve with a side dish of spiced sauce made by mixing together the chilli sauce, fresh grated ginger, soya sauce, garlic juice and sugar.

Smoked Duck photographed at **Hin's Heavenly Cookhouse,** Hilton Hotel

Onion Duck

1 duck, about 1.5 kilos
3 large brown onions
3 spring onions
25 ml light soya sauce
50 ml Chinese wine
100 ml vegetable oil
250 ml chicken stock
2 teaspoons brown sugar
½ teaspoon salt
¼ teaspoon white pepper
25 g cornstarch

serves 6

Prepare and wash the duck and dry thoroughly inside and outside. Slice the brown onions and chop the spring onions. Mix the onions with the soya sauce and half the Chinese wine, stuff the mixture into the cavity of the duck and secure with thread. Heat the oil in a wok, add the duck and fry over a moderately hot heat for 10 minutes, turning occasionally to ensure an even goldness to the skin. Then remove the duck, drain off all excess oil and place into a large saucepean. Pour in the stock together with a similar quantity of cold water. Bring to the boil then add the remaining Chinese wine, the sugar, salt and white pepper. Place a tightly fitting lid on the pan, lower heat and allow to simmer for approximately 1½ hours until the duck is cooked. Then remove the duck, drain and transfer to a serving dish. Increase the heat under the saucepan and rapidly reduce the stock by half. Mix the cornstarch with a small quantity of cold water and stir into the sauce to thicken to a desired consistency then pour over the duck and serve immediately.

Duckling with Lotus Seed Stuffing

1 fat duckling, about 1.5 kilos
1 teaspoon salt
freshly ground black pepper
oil for deep frying
6 black Chinese mushrooms
125 g lean pork meat
20 mm knob fresh ginger
3 spring onions
100 g lotus seeds
4 yolks of preserved duck eggs
25 ml light soya sauce
25 ml dark soya sauce
pinch monosodium glutamate

Sauce:
75 ml chicken stock
2 teaspoons light soya sauce
2 teaspoons Chinese wine
1 teaspoon seasame oil
1 teaspoon sugar
¼ teaspoon white pepper
salt to taste

serves 6

Clean, prepare and bone the duckling. Dry thoroughly and rub the inside and outside with salt and freshly ground black pepper. Heat the oil in a large wok and deep fry the duckling for a few minutes until the skin is crispy and golden. Chop the mushrooms, pork, ginger, spring onions and lotus seeds and mix with the duck egg yolks, soya sauce and monosodium glutamate. Stuff the mixture into the cavity of the duckling, place in a steamer and cook for 1¼ hours. Finally pour the prepared sauce over the duckling and continue to steam until the duck is well cooked, approximately a further 15 minutes.

To prepare the sauce mix together all the ingredients, bring to the boil and simmer for 2–3 minutes before pouring over the duckling.

Serve with sauteed Chinese vegetables.

Boneless Duck

1 fat duck, about 1.5 kilos
1 teaspoon salt
½ teaspoon white pepper
½ teaspoon Chinese five-spice powder
pinch monosodium glutamate
2 teaspoons fresh lime juice
1 teaspoon vinegar
100 g honey
25 ml peanut oil

Sauce:
2 shallots
1 clove garlic
1 square beancurd
1 teaspoon plum sauce
1 teaspoon vinegar
1 teaspoon sugar
salt to taste
freshly ground black pepper
100 ml chicken stock

serves 6

Clean and prepare the duck, carefully removing all the bones. Mix together the salt, white pepper, five-spice powder and monosodium glutamate and rub the mixture inside the duck. In a large saucepan bring 500 ml of water to the boil, add the lime juice, vinegar and honey and stir to blend thoroughly. Allow the syrup to cool then rub evenly over the skin of the duck and hang the duck in a warm and draughty place for 3–4 hours. Place the duck in a roasting pan, add the peanut oil and cook in a moderately hot oven for approximately 1½ hours, turning occasionally to ensure the skin becomes crispy and golden all over. Remove the duck from the pan, slice the meat and arrange on a serving plate.

To make the sauce, chop the shallots, garlic and beancurd and add these to the roasting pan. Place the pan over a moderate heat and sauté the vegetable for 2–3 minutes then add the plum sauce, vinegar and sugar and season to taste with salt and freshly ground black pepper. Pour in the stock and bring to the boil. Lower heat, simmer gently for 3 minutes then pour the sauce over the duck.

Quail Curry

8 fresh quails
1 teaspoon salt
½ teaspoon white pepper
6 shallots
20 mm knob fresh ginger
2 cloves garlic
2 large tomatoes
4 green cardamon seeds
4 black cardamon seeds
20 mm stick cinnamon
100 g ghee
2 teaspoons chilli powder
1 teaspoon turmeric powder
1 teaspoon cumin powder
½ teaspoon saffron powder
150 ml plain yoghurt

Clean and prepare the quails and season with salt and freshly ground white pepper. Chop the shallots, ginger, garlic and tomatoes and grind the cardamon seeds and cinnamon. Heat the ghee in a large saucepan and sauté the shallots for 2–3 minutes then add the ginger, garlic and tomato and stir well. Add the quails and cook for a further 2 minutes, turning occasionally. Add all the spices and continue to cook for 5 minutes, stirring frequently to avoid sticking. Finally pour in the yoghurt together with 100 ml of water and bring to the boil. Cover the pan, lower heat and simmer until the quails are fully cooked and the sauce has thickened. Serve with raisin rice.

Meats

Lamb Madras

400 g fresh lamb
150 ml natural yoghurt
2 large boiled potatoes
2 large brown onions
2 large tomatoes
2 fresh red chillies
20 mm knob fresh ginger
3 cloves garlic
25 g ghee
2 teaspoons coriander powder
2 teaspoons cumin powder
2 teaspoons turmeric powder
50 g tomato paste
150 ml thick coconut milk
50 g cooked green peas
salt to taste

serves 4

Chop the meat into very small pieces, place in a shallow dish, cover with the yoghurt and set aside for 1 hour. Dice the potatoes, slice the onions and tomatoes, chop the chillies and ginger and crush the garlic. Heat the ghee in a large pan and saute the onion, chilli, ginger and garlic for 3–4 minutes. Add the lamb together with the yoghurt, bring to the boil slowly and simmer for 8 minutes. Then add the coriander, cumin and turmeric powders, tomato, tomato paste and coconut milk and bring back to the boil. Cook for a further 3–4 minutes, stirring continuously, then add the diced potato and the peas and season to taste with salt. Stir to blend thoroughly and continue to simmer until the potato is heated through then transfer to a serving dish.

Lamb Madras photographed at **Hin's Heavenly Cookhouse,** Hilton Hotel

Sweet & Sour Pork photographed at **Shang Palace,** Shangri La Hotel

Sweet and Sour Pork

400 g fresh pork tenderloin
½ teaspoon salt
¼ teaspoon white pepper
¼ teaspoon Chinese five-spice powder
pinch monosodium glutamate
2 eggs
25 ml Chinese wine
25 ml light soya sauce
50 g cornstarch
oil for deep frying

Sauce:
1 brown onion
1 green pepper
1 large tomato
2 carrots
30 mm length cucumber
2 fresh red chillies
15 mm knob fresh ginger
1 clove garlic
200 ml chicken stock
25 ml Chinese wine
25 ml light soya sauce
2 teaspoons dark soya sauce
25 ml vinegar
25 ml fresh lemon juice
25 g tomato sauce
50 g sugar
75 g canned pineapple chunks
2 teaspoons cornstarch

serves 4

Cut the pork into bite size pieces and season with salt, white pepper, five-spice powder and monosodium glutamate. Beat the eggs, add the Chinese wine and soya sauce and pour over the pork. Allow the meat to marinate for 30 minutes then remove and coat with the cornstarch. Heat the oil in a wok and when very hot, deep-fry the pork until it is thoroughly cooked and the outside is golden and crispy. Pour away most of the oil and set the meat aside to drain.

Chop the onion, green pepper and tomato fairly coarsely, slice the carrots and cucumber, cut the chillies and ginger into julienne strips and crush the garlic. Place the wok over a high heat and stir-fry the vegetables for 1–2 minutes then add the stock, Chinese wine, soya sauce, vinegar, fresh lemon juice, tomato sauce and sugar and bring to the boil. Stir to blend thoroughly and to dissolve the sugar then add the chunks of pineapple, lower the heat and allow to simmer gently for 3 minutes. Mix the cornstarch with a small quantity of cold water and stir into the sauce to thicken slightly. Arrange the pork on a large serving plate, pour the sauce on top and serve immediately.

Rogan Josh

800 g boned mutton
2 large brown onions
25 mm knob fresh ginger
3 cloves garlic
2 large tomatoes
2 squares beancurd
2 black cardamon seeds
2 green cardamon seeds
3 cloves
2 bay leaves
20 mm stick cinnamon
100 g ghee
150 ml plain yoghurt
salt to taste
25 g coriander powder
2 teaspoons cumin powder
1 teaspoon chilli powder
½ teaspoon white pepper
1 teaspoon chopped parsley

serves 6

Trim excess fat from the mutton and cut into cubes. Chop the onions and the ginger, crush the garlic and dice the tomatoes and beancurd. Make a spice bag by wrapping the cardamon seeds, cloves, bay leaves and cinnamon in fine muslin. Heat the ghee in a large pan and fry the onion until golden then add the ginger and garlic and stir-fry for 5 minutes. Add the tomatoes, beancurd, yoghurt, salt and spice bag. Then add the meat and cook slowly for 10 minutes, stirring frequently. Add the coriander, cumin, chilli and white pepper and continue to cook for a further 15 minutes then pour in 1 litre of cold water and bring to the boil. Lower heat and cook until the meat is tender, approximately 35 minutes. Remove the spice bag, transfer to a serving dish and sprinkle the chopped parsley on top.

Lamb Apple Korma

600 g boned lamb
2 cooking apples
2 large brown onions
2 large ripe tomatoes
3 cloves garlic
50 g ghee
2 teaspoons coriander powder
2 teaspoons cumin powder
1 teaspoon chilli powder
25 g ground cashewnuts
75 ml plain yoghurt
salt to taste
freshly ground white pepper
50 ml fresh cream

serves 4

Trim excess fat from lamb and cut into cubes. Peel and dice the apples and onions, mash the tomatoes and finely chop the garlic. Heat the ghee in a frying pan, add the onion and fry until golden. Then add the tomato, garlic, coriander and cumin and stir-fry for 5 minutes. Add the chilli powder and ground cashewnuts and cook for a further 3 minutes then pour in the yoghurt and season to taste with salt and freshly ground white pepper. Simmer for 5 minutes, stirring frequently, then add the lamb, pour in 200 ml of cold water and bring to the boil. Lower heat and cook slowly until the lamb is tender, approximately 45 minutes, then add the apple and cook for another 5 minutes. Finally, remove from heat, stir in the cream and serve immediately.

Mutton Shish Kebab

400 g fresh mutton
1 teaspoon salt
½ teaspoon white pepper
2 shallots
2 fresh red chillies
1 fresh green chilli
20 mm knob fresh ginger
4 cloves garlic
2 teaspoons chopped parsley
1 teaspoon chopped mint
¼ teaspoon powdered mace
2 teaspoons curry powder
50 g soft white breadcrumbs
25 ml tomato ketchup
25 ml fresh lemon juice
kebab sticks

Date sauce:
100 g dates
1 shallot
1 fresh red chilli
1 clove garlic
25 g soft brown sugar
25 ml chilli sauce
salt to taste
freshly ground black pepper

serves 4–6

Mince the mutton and season to taste with salt and white pepper. Chop the shallots, chillies and ginger very finely and crush the garlic. Place the vegetables in a stone mortar and pound to a smooth paste. Transfer to a large mixing bowl, break in the egg, add the mutton, parsley, mint, mace, curry powder, breadcrumbs, tomato ketchup and lemon juice and blend thoroughly. Dip the wooden kebab sticks in cold water and wet the hands then take a little of the mixture and shape it around a stick like a long thin sausage roll, about 15 mm thick and 100 mm in length. Press slightly with the hands. When all the kebabs have been prepared cook over a hot charcoal fire or under a grill until the meat is well cooked. Serve with the prepared date sauce.

To make the sauce remove the stones from the dates and pass through a fine mincer. Chop the shallot, chilli, garlic and mint and pound these together with the dates. Add the brown sugar, chilli sauce, salt and pepper to taste and 75 ml of cold water. Continue to pound until the ingredients are thoroughly blended and the sauce is thick and smooth. Add a little more water if a thinner sauce is preferred. Serve as a dip for the kebabs.

Spiced Mutton Chops

450 g mutton chops
25 ml Worcestershire sauce
2 teaspoons dark soya sauce
4 shallots
2 fresh red chillies
1 fresh green chilli
20 mm knob fresh ginger
3 cloves garlic
2 teaspoons curry powder
1 teaspoon coriander powder
25 ml peanut oil
salt to taste
freshly ground black pepper
ghee for frying

serves 4

Trim the excess fat from the chops and place in a shallow dish. Pour the Worcestershire sauce and soya sauce over the chops and set aside for 1 hour. Chop the shallots, chillies, ginger and garlic and pound together with the curry powder, coriander powder and peanut oil. Place the spice paste in a heavy saucepan and stir-fry for 2 minutes, then add the chops, season to taste with salt and freshly ground black pepper and pour in just sufficient cold water to prevent the chops from sticking. Stir well then cover the pan and cook over a low heat until the chops are tender and the liquid has dried up. Just prior to serving heat the ghee in a frying pan and fry the chops for 2 minutes, turning once. Serve with steamed rice and a green salad.

Oven Smoked Spare Ribs

1 kilo pork ribs
2 fresh red chillies
15 mm knob fresh ginger
1 clove garlic
1 square preserved beancurd
25 ml light soya sauce
25 ml sweet & sour sauce
50 g sugar
salt to taste
freshly ground white pepper
50 ml chilli sauce

serves 4–6

Place the pork in a large shallow dish with the fat side facing upwards. Chop the chillies, ginger and garlic and pound together with the beancurd, soya sauce, sweet & sour sauce, sugar, salt and freshly ground white pepper. Pour the mixture over the ribs, place in the refrigerator and allow to marinate for 24 hours. After marination hang the pork on hooks and cook in a very hot charcoal oven for 25 minutes then remove, brush with the chilli sauce and return to the oven for a further 5 minutes. Remove the pork again and this time brush with the remaining marinade. Return to the oven for another 5 minutes or until the pork is fully cooked.

Note: If a charcoal oven is not available, cook the pork on a rack over a charcoal fire taking care to retain an even heat. When using this method turn the meat occasionally and baste with the sauce and marinade as above.

Special Fried Spare Ribs

1 kilo pork ribs
2 eggs
50 ml ginger juice
50 ml Chinese wine
½ teaspoon Chinese five-spice powder
100 g cornstarch
½ teaspoon salt
¼ teaspoon white pepper
pinch monosodium glutamate
oil for deep frying
2 brown onions
100 g tomato sauce
75 ml Worcester sauce
25 ml light soya sauce
25 ml dark soya sauce
100 g fine white sugar

serves 4–6

Trim the excess fat from the ribs and cut into individual bones. Tap the bones lightly with the back of a knife (this loosens the meat a little), cut each rib into two and place in a shallow dish. Beat the egg, add the ginger juice, Chinese wine, five-spice powder, all but 2 teaspoons of the cornstarch, salt, pepper and monosodium glutamate and pour the mixture over the pork. Allow to stand for 1 hour, turning the ribs occasionally. Heat the oil in a large pan until it starts to smoke then add the ribs and deep fry for 3 minutes. Then strain, discard the oil and set the ribs aside. Chop the onion and add to the pan. Lower heat and saute for 2–3 minutes. Add the tomato sauce, Worcester sauce, soya sauce and sugar and bring to the boil. Replace the ribs and adjust seasonings to taste. Mix the remaining cornstarch with a small quantity of cold water and add to the sauce. Bring back to the boil, stir well and allow to simmer for a further minute then serve immediately.

Spare Ribs photographed at **Hin's Heavenly Cookhouse**, Hilton Hotel

Singapore Meat Satay

400 g beef or mutton
4 shallots
2 cloves garlic
4 stalks lemon grass
20 mm knob fresh ginger
1 teaspoon coriander powder
1 teaspoon cumin powder
2 teaspoons sugar
salt to taste
freshly ground black pepper
peanut oil for basting

Satay sauce:
8 dried red chillies
2 cloves garlic
4 shallots
4 candlenuts (or macadamia nuts)
25 ml thick coconut milk
50 ml peanut oil
150 g peanuts
50 ml tamarind water (or fresh
lemon juice)
25 g sugar
salt to taste
freshly ground black pepper

serves 4–6

Cut the meat into small thin strips, about 50 mm × 20 mm. Chop the shallots, garlic, lemon grass and ginger and place in a stone mortar and pound together with the coriander and cumin. Transfer to a large bowl, add the meat, the sugar, salt, freshly ground black pepper and 50 ml of cold water. Mix with a wooden spoon to blend thoroughly and set aside for 1½ hours. When marinaded place the meat on wooden skewers (3 or 4 pieces to each skewer) and cook over a hot charcoal fire, basting frequently with the peanut oil. Serve with slices of raw onion, wedges of cucumber and satay sauce.

To make the sauce: first soak the chillies in cold water until they become soft then chop finely. Chop the garlic, shallots, and macadamia nuts. Grind all these ingredients together with the coconut milk. Heat the oil in a large pan and stir-fry the spice paste for 5 minutes. Then chop the peanuts very finely and add these to the pan together with the tamarind water, 150 ml of cold water, the sugar, salt and freshly ground black pepper. Bring to the boil then lower heat and simmer slowly until the sauce thickens to a desired consistency.

Fried Shredded Beef with Peppers

250 g lean beef
1 medium size green pepper
2 fresh red chillies
1 egg
50 ml light soya sauce
50 ml Chinese wine
25 g cornstarch
½ teaspoon salt
¼ teaspoon white pepper
pinch monosodium glutamate
50 ml vegetable oil
25 ml Chicken stock

serve 4

Cut the beef into small thin slices and place in a shallow dish. Cut the green pepper and chillies into strips. Beat the egg and mix with half the soya sauce, half the Chinese wine, the cornstarch, salt, white pepper and monosodium glutamate. Pour the mixture over the meat and set aside for 30 minutes. Heat half the oil in a wok, add the meat together with the marinade and cook over a moderate heat for 3–4 minutes until the meat is well browned. Then remove the beef, drain and set aside. Next heat the remaining oil in the wok and sauté the pepper and chilli for 1 minute. Pour in the remaining soya sauce, Chinese wine and the stock and adjust seasonings to taste. Bring to the boil, add the beef and stir fry for a further 30 seconds before transferring to a serving dish.

Sautéed Beef in Oyster Sauce

400 g lean beef
2 teaspoons cornstarch
25 ml Chinese wine
25 ml light soya sauce
2 teaspoons dark soya sauce
½ teaspoon salt
¼ teaspoon white pepper
pinch monosodium glutamate
2 shallots
2 cloves garlic
50 ml peanut oil
25 ml oyster sauce

serves 4

Cut the meat into thin, bite-size slices and place in a shallow dish. Mix the cornstarch with the Chinese wine and the soya sauce and season with the salt, white pepper and monosodium glutamate. Pour the mixture over the beef ensuring that it is evenly coated then set aside for 30 minutes. Chop the shallots and garlic finely. Heat half the oil in a wok and sauté the shallot and garlic until it is golden and crispy then remove and set aside. Add the remaining oil to the wok and place over a high heat. Add the beef and sauté for 2–3 minutes, stirring frequently, then replace the shallot and garlic and pour in the oyster sauce together with 50 ml of water. Simmer for a further 2 minutes then serve immediately.

Fried Beef with Noodles

400 g lean beef
6 shallots
2 fresh red chillies
2 spring onions
20 mm knob fresh ginger
200 g egg noodles
100 ml vegetable oil
2 teaspoons light soya sauce
2 teaspoons Chinese wine
salt to taste
freshly ground black pepper

serves 4

Cut the meat into thin slices, about 50 mm × 15 mm. Chop the shallots, chillies, spring onions and ginger. Cook the noodles in rapidly boiling salted water until tender, drain thoroughly, then spread out and set aside in a warm place to dry. Heat half the oil in a wok, add the noodles and fry for 2–3 minutes, stirring frequently. Remove the noodles from the pan, drain then arrange on a serving plate and keep warm. Pour the remaining oil in to the wok and place over a high heat then add the beef, the vegetables, the soya sauce and Chinese wine and season to taste with salt and freshly ground black pepper. Stir-fry for 3–4 minutes until the meat is well cooked then arrange on top of the noodles and serve immediately.

Venison with Ginger and Spring Onions

500 g venison meat
½ teaspoon salt
¼ teaspoon white pepper
¼ teaspoon bicarbonate of soda
25 mm knob fresh ginger
3 spring onions
25 ml vegetable oil
lettuce leaves
2 teaspoons light soya sauce
2 teaspoons oyster sauce
2 teaspoons peanut oil
1 teaspoon sugar

serves 4–6

Cut the meat into small thin slices and season with the salt, white pepper and bicarbonate of soda. Cut the ginger into fine julienne strips and chop the spring onions. Heat the oil in a small saucepan and sauté the ginger and spring onion for 2–3 minutes. Line an earthenware pot with crispy lettuce leaves and place the slices of meat on top. Add the ginger, spring onion, soya sauce, oyster sauce, peanut oil and sugar and place a tightly fitting lid on pot. Cook over a low heat for 3–4 minutes then increase heat and cook for a further 3–4 minutes until the meat is tender.

Local Favourites

Chilli Crab

3 large fresh water crabs
4–6 fresh red chillies
20 mm knob fresh ginger
2 cloves garlic
100 ml vegetable oil
25 g sugar
salt to taste
freshly ground black pepper
pinch monosodium glutamate
300 ml chicken stock
2 teaspoons vinegar
2 teaspoons light soya sauce
25 g tomato sauce
1 egg
chunks of white bread

serves 4–6

Scrub the crabs with a stiff brush and rinse well under cold running water. Remove the claws and smash slightly. Chop the crab-backs into medium size pieces taking care to discard the grey and pulpy matter. Chop the chillies, ginger and garlic. Heat the oil in a wok and cook the crabs for 1–2 minutes, stirring frequently, then remove the crabs to the side of the wok and pour off most of the oil. Add the chilli, ginger and garlic and sauté for 2–3 minutes then return the crab to the heat, add the sugar, salt, freshly ground black pepper and monosodium glutamate and pour in the stock. Stir well then bring to the boil, cover the pan and simmer slowly until the crab is cooked, approximately 15 minutes. Remove the cover and add the vinegar, soya sauce and tomato sauce. Beat the egg lightly, add this to the sauce and stir for a further minute until the egg begins to set and the sauce thickens slightly. Serve with chunks of white bread for eating with the sauce.

Chilli Crab photographed at **Cathay Restaurant**

Hainanese Chicken Rice photographed at **Waterfall Cafe,** Shangri La Hotel

Hainanese Chicken Rice

1 fresh chicken, about 1.25 kilos
salt
300 g long grain rice
50 mm piece cucumber
2 tomatoes
6 shallots
4 fresh red chillies
20 mm knob fresh ginger
1 clove garlic
fresh parsley leaves
freshly ground black pepper

serves 4

Clean and prepare the chicken, rub the outside and the inside with salt and set aside for 1 hour. Wash the rice under cold running water and allow to drain. Cut the cucumber and tomatoes into tiny dice, chop the shallots, chillies and ginger and crush the garlic. In a large saucepan bring 1 litre of water to the boil, add the ginger and garlic and allow to boil rapidly for 3–4 minutes. Add the chicken and the parsley leaves, cover the pan, lower heat and simmer until the chicken is tender. Remove a little oil from the surface of the stock and set aside. Remove the chicken, cut into small portions and arrange on a serving platter. Heat the reserved oil in a wok and saute the shallot for 3–4 minutes then pour in half the stock, add the cucumber, tomato and chilli, season to taste with salt and freshly ground black pepper and bring to the boil. Cover the pan, lower heat and simmer slowly for 20–25 minutes. In the meantime bring the stock remaining in the saucepan back to the boil, add the rice and cook until tender. Serve the rice and soup in individual bowls and place the platter of chicken in the centre. Serve with side dishes of ginger and garlic sauce, hot chilli sauce and soya sauce.

Fish Head Curry

1 large fish head
25 g dried tamarind
2 large brown onions
2 large tomatoes
4 fresh red chillies
2 fresh green chillies
25 mm knob fresh ginger
2 cloves garlic
75 g curry powder
50 ml vegetable oil
2 sprigs curry leaves
400 ml thin coconut milk
salt to taste

serves 2

Wash the fish head under cold running water and pat dry. Place the tamarind in 150 ml of cold water and set aside for 1 hour then strain through fine muslin, discard the tamarind and retain the water. Slice the onions, quarter the tomatoes and finely chop the chillies, ginger and garlic. Mix the curry powder with a small quantity of cold water to form a smooth paste. Heat the oil in a large pan and fry the onion, ginger and garlic for 2–3 minutes then add the chillies and continue to cook for a further 3 minutes, stirring frequently. Next add the curry paste and the curry leaves, cover the pan and cook over a moderate heat for 2 minutes, then remove the lid and slowly pour in the tamarind water and the coconut, stirring to blend thoroughly. When simmering add the fish head and the tomatoes and season to taste with salt. Cook for 8–10 minutes over a moderate heat until the fish is completely cooked. Transfer the fish head to a serving plate and keep warm. Increase heat under the pan and reduce the sauce by one quarter then pour this over the fish and serve immediately with plain rice.

Note: In many 'Western' kitchens the fish head is used only for stock, or indeed may often be wastefully discarded, yet here is to be found some of the tastiest meat on the fish. So even though fish fillets could simply be substituted by the unadventurous for a similar result the recipe is highly recommended in its original form.

Sotong Ayam

8 medium size cuttlefish
400 g cooked chicken meat
2 shallots
2 spring onions
2 fresh red chillies
1 teaspoon blachan (spiced shrimp paste)
2 teaspoons peanut oil
2 teaspoons sugar
salt to taste
pinch monosodium glutamate
250 ml thick coconut milk
2 teaspoons sesame oil

serves 4

Clean the cuttlefish and remove the head and the backbone. Chop the chicken meat finely, season to taste and stuff into the cuttlefish cavities. Chop the shallots, spring onions, chillies and blachan and pound these together. Heat the oil in a small pan and fry the pounded ingredients for 3 minutes then add the sugar, salt and monosodium glutamate and stir to blend thoroughly. Add the coconut milk, bring to simmering point and stir well for a further 2–3 minutes. Finally add the stuffed cuttlefish, cover the pan and simmer over a moderate heat for approximately 15 minutes. Transfer to a serving plate and sprinkle with hot sesame oil.

Orr Chien

200 g small fresh oysters
2 teaspoons Chinese wine
freshly ground black pepper
1 spring onion
1 fresh red chilli
1 clove garlic
few celery leaves
50 g rice flour
salt
3 eggs
vegetable oil
2 teaspoons light soya sauce
1 teaspoon dark soya sauce

serves 4

Wash the oysters under cold running water then allow to drain. Season the oysters with Chinese wine and freshly ground black pepper and set aside for 20 minutes. Chop the spring onion, chilli, garlic and celery leaves very finely. Mix the flour and $\frac{1}{4}$ teaspoon of salt with 150 ml of warm water. Beat the eggs in a separate bowl. Heat the oil in a wok until it is very hot then add the batter and the egg. Stir to blend and allow to set slightly, breaking the mixture up with a spatula, then remove to the side of the wok. Add the oysters, onion, chilli, garlic and celery leaves and stir fry for 2–3 minutes. Add the soya sauce and additional salt and pepper to taste, bring the egg mixture back to the centre of the wok, stir to blend thoroughly and continue to cook until the egg is set.

Hokkien Fried Noodles

500 g yellow flour noodles
200 g bean sprouts
200 g small fresh prawns
100 g boiled squid
100 g boiled pork
6 fresh red chillies
2 spring onions
2 cloves garlic
50 ml peanut oil
50 ml chicken stock
salt to taste
freshly ground black pepper
2 teaspoons dark soya sauce
2 eggs
25 ml fresh milk

serves 4–6

Soak the noodles in a bowl of very hot water for 30 seconds then pour into a colander and allow to drain thoroughly. Wash the bean sprouts under cold running water and remove the skins and small roots. Shell and de-vein the prawns and cut into half lengthways. Cut the squid and pork into thin strips. Chop the chillies and spring onions and crush the garlic. Heat half the oil in a wok and saute the garlic for 1 minute then add the chilli, prawns, squid and pork and continue to stir-fry over a moderate heat for a further 3 minutes, placing a cover on the wok for the last minute. Then remove the cover, pour in the stock, add the spring onion and season to taste with salt and freshly ground black pepper. Bring to the boil, add the bean sprouts and stir for 1 minute. Add the remaining oil, the soya sauce and the noodles and stir to blend thoroughly. Replace the cover on the wok and cook for 30 seconds then transfer to a serving dish. Beat the eggs with the milk and pour into the wok. Place over a moderate heat and when the egg is set cut into thin strips and place on top of the noodles.

Tauhu Goreng photographed at **Waterfall Cafe,** Shangri La Hotel

Tauhu Goreng

**6 squares beancurd
oil for deep frying
250 g bean sprouts
1 small cucumber**

**Peanut sauce:
1 teaspoon chopped garlic
50 ml peanut oil
2 teaspoons ground chilli
300 g ground roasted peanuts
25 ml vinegar
2 teaspoons fresh lime juice
2 teaspoons dark soya sauce
25 g soft brown sugar
salt to taste**

serves 4

Heat the oil until almost smoking and deep fry the beancurd until golden brown. Then slice and arrange on a serving plate. Wash the bean sprouts, pluck off any roots and par-boil in a pan of rapidly boiling water. Remove, drain thoroughly and place on top of the beancurd. Slice the cucumber and arrange around the edge of the plate. Pour warm peanut sauce on top and serve immediately.

To make the sauce: heat the peanut oil in a saucepan and first fry the chopped garlic until it is crispy and golden. Remove the garlic and allow to drain. Mix together the chopped chilli, ground peanuts, garlic, vinegar, lime juice, soya sauce, sugar and salt. Re-heat the peanut oil and stir-fry the mixture for 5 minutes then add 100 ml of water and bring to the boil. Lower heat and simmer for 2–3 minutes, stirring frequently. Allow the sauce to cool slightly before pouring on to the vegetables.

Beef Rendang

400 g lean beef
6 shallots
20 mm knob fresh ginger
1 clove garlic
4 dried red chillies
2 teaspoons peanut oil
50 ml vegetable oil
1 teaspoon sugar
50 g grated coconut
250 ml thick coconut milk
salt to taste

serves 4

Cut the beef into bite size pieces. Chop the shallots, ginger, garlic and chillies and pound together with the peanut oil to form a smooth paste. Heat the vegetable oil in a pan and fry the spice paste for 3–4 minutes, stirring frequently. Add the beef and continue to cook over a medium heat for a further 3 minutes then add the sugar, grated coconut and coconut milk and bring to the boil. Lower heat, add salt to taste and simmer slowly until the beef is tender and most of the liquid has been absorbed. Serve with boiled rice or saffron rice.

Beef Rendang photographed at **The Islander Restaurant,** Hyatt Hotel

Desserts

Bo Bo Cha Cha

400 g yams (sweet potatoes)
50 g powdered gelatine
300 g fine white sugar
½ teaspoon red food colouring
½ teaspoon green food colouring
shaved ice
500 g thick coconut milk

serves 6

Peel the yams, cut into 15 mm cubes and cook in boiling water for 15 minutes. Drain in a colander and set aside to cool. Dissolve the gelatine powder in a small quantity of boiling water. In a saucepan bring 1 litre of water to the boil, add the gelatine and half the sugar. Stir until the sugar has completely dissolved then pour equal amounts into two separate bowls and mix the red colouring into one and the green into the other. Allow to cool then place in the refrigerator to set firmly. In a clean saucepan bring a further 250 ml of water to the boil, add the remaining sugar, stir to dissolve then set aside to cool.

To serve, cut the jellies into small cubes and place a little of each colour into individual tall sundae glasses. Add the yam and then the remaining jelly. Add the syrup, fill up the glasses with shaved ice and pour the coconut milk on top.

Szechuan Pancakes

2 eggs
100 g all-purpose flour
25 g melted butter
75 ml fresh milk
2 teaspoons fine white sugar
½ teaspoon vanilla essence
peanut oil
1 teaspoon finely ground almonds

Filling:
100 g Chinese red dates
150 g sweet bean paste
1 teaspoon Chinese wine
1 teaspoon fine white sugar

serves 6–8

Break the eggs into a mixing bowl, add the flour, butter, milk, sugar and vanilla essence and beat to blend thoroughly. Add just sufficient cold water to make a thin creamy batter. Heat some of the oil in a large frying pan until it is very hot then pour in a little of the batter. Tilt the pan so that the batter spreads out into a thin, large circle. Allow the batter to set slightly then add a portion of the prepared filling, spread it evenly, then fold to form a long rectangular shape. Seal folds with a little batter and continue to cook, turning once, until the pancake is golden and the outside is crispy. Remove to a wire rack and keep warm. Continue to prepare pancakes until all the batter and filling has been used up, adding a little more oil to the pan each time. When all the pancakes have been prepared, cut crossways into small 'fingers', arrange on a serving plate and sprinkle the finely ground almond on top.

To prepare the filling, mash the dates with a little cold water. Add the sweet bean paste and the sugar and stir to blend thoroughly.

Koulfi Pista

600 ml fresh milk
50 ml fresh cream
50 g fine white sugar
2 eggs
1 teaspoon rose water
2 teaspoons ground almonds
25 g finely chopped pistachio nuts

serves 4

In a heavy saucepan heat the milk and reduce by half. Add the cream and sugar and stir over a moderate heat until the sugar has completely dissolved. Separate the eggs and add the yolks to the milk mixture together with the rose water and the ground almonds. Keep at simmering point and beat well for 4–5 minutes. Then remove from the heat and allow to cool slightly. Pour the mixture into chilled ice-cream trays, place in the freezer and leave until three-quarters set. Then remove from the freezer, beat the egg whites until stiff and fold into the mixture. Place back in the freezer until completely set then transfer to individual glasses and serve immediately.

Payasam

200 g sago
50 g thin rice noodles
50 g unsalted cashew nuts, shelled
50 g sultanas
150 ml thick coconut milk
150 castor sugar
pinch of salt
1 teaspoon rose essence

serves 4

Wash the sago under cold running water and drain well. Pour 250 ml of water into a saucepan and place over moderate heat. When the water is just at the boil, sprinkle in the sago and simmer until the sago becomes transparent. Wash the noodles, cashew nuts and sultanas, add these to the sago and continue to simmer for 7–8 minutes. Then add the coconut milk, sugar and salt, bring back to the boil and stir until the sugar has completely dissolved. Serve into individual dishes and sprinkle a little rose essence on top of each. Serve either hot or cold.

Peanut Pudding

150 g fresh peanuts
75 ml peanut oil
150 g cornstarch
50 ml Carnation milk
150 g granulated white sugar
2 teaspoons soft brown sugar

serves 4

Heat the oil in a pan and stir-fry the peanuts for 3 minutes then pour into a colander and allow to cool. Remove husks from the peanuts and grind very finely. Mix the cornstarch with a small quantity of cold water. In a saucepan heat 750 ml of water and when just coming to the boil add the ground peanut and stir. Add the cornstarch, Carnation milk and sugar and simmer over a moderate heat for 4 minutes, stirring frequently. Transfer to individual serving dishes and sprinkle a little brown sugar on top.

Rum Raisin Ice-Cream photographed at **Hilton Hotel**

Rum Raisin Ice-Cream in Coconut

1 fresh vanilla stick
400 ml fresh milk
1 egg
5 egg-whites
125 g fine white sugar
100 ml fresh cream
100 ml dark rum
150 g seedless raisins
4 young coconuts
25 g grated coconut

serves 4

Slice the vanilla stick and with a knife remove the seeds. Pour the milk into a saucepan, add the vanilla seeds and bring to the boil. Beat the egg and egg-whites together with the sugar and add to the milk. Continue to simmer until the mixture thickens but do not allow to come to the boil again. Remove the pan from the heat, stir in the cream and allow the mixture to cool then strain through a fine muslin cloth into an ice-cream tray. Place in the freezer compartment and when half set remove and fold in the rum and two-thirds of the raisins. Return to the freezer until completely set. To serve: remove the tops from the coconuts, pour away any liquid and place scoops of ice-cream inside. Sprinkle the grated coconut and the remaining raisins on top.

Pisang Goreng Mas

8 small bananas
75 g all-purpose flour
25 g butter
2 teaspoons lemon juice
2 teaspoons orange juice
25 g fine white sugar
25 g grated coconut

serves 4

Peel the bananas and cut into quarters, first lengthways then across. Mix the flour with sufficient water to form a thin batter and coat the pieces of banana. Melt the butter in a frying pan and fry the banana pieces until golden on one side. Then turn over, add the lemon and orange juice and continue to cook until golden all over. Transfer to a serving dish and sprinkle the sugar and grated coconut on top.

Pisang Goreng Mas photographed at **The Islander Restaurant,** Hyatt Hotel

Index

Listed below are the restaurants and hotels from which most of the recipes in this edition were obtained. Thanks are due to all personnel involved. Where photographs were taken additional acknowledgements appear on the appropriate pages:
CATHAY RESTAURANT; CENTURY PARK SHERATON HOTEL; DRAGON PALACE (Cockpit Hotel); GOLDEN PHOENIX (Equatorial Hotel); GOODWOOD PARK HOTEL; GREAT SHANGHAI RESTAURANT; GUAN HOE SOON RESTAURANT; HIN'S HEAVENLY COOKHOUSE (Hilton Hotel); THE ISLANDER (Hyatt Hotel); LUNA COFFEE SHOP (Apollo Hotel); MAJESTIC RESTAURANT; MANDARIN COURT (Mandarin Hotel); MING PALACE (Ming Court Hotel); OMEI RESTAURANT; PEKING RESTAURANT; SHALIMAR RESTAURANT; SHANG PALACE (Shangri La Hotel); RANG MAHAL (Imperial Hotel); UJAGAH SINGH'S; WATERFALL CAFE (Shangri La Hotel).